Dog Vaccination

Schedule

Pet Name:_____ Date of birth:_____

Breed:_____

Vaccine	Immunization Dates						Veterinarian
Ardenovirus-2							
Bordetella							
Coronavirus							
Distemper							
Heartworm							
Hepatitis							
Leptospirosis							
Lyme Disease							
Parainfluenza							
Parvovirus							
Rabies							

Notes:

Pet Name:_____ Date of birth:_____

Breed:_____

Vaccine	Immunization Dates						Veterinarian
Ardenovirus-2							
Bordetella							
Coronavirus							
Distemper							
Heartworm							
Hepatitis							
Leptospirosis							
Lyme Disease							
Parainfluenza							
Parvovirus							
Rabies							

Notes:

Pet Name:_____ Date of birth:_____

Breed:_____

Vaccine	Immunization Dates						Veterinarian
Ardenovirus-2							
Bordetella							
Coronavirus							
Distemper							
Heartworm							
Hepatitis							
Leptospirosis							
Lyme Disease							
Parainfluenza							
Parvovirus							
Rabies							

Notes:

Pet Name:_____ Date of birth:_____

Breed:_____

Vaccine	Immunization Dates						Veterinarian
Ardenovirus-2							
Bordetella							
Coronavirus							
Distemper							
Heartworm							
Hepatitis							
Leptospirosis							
Lyme Disease							
Parainfluenza							
Parvovirus							
Rabies							

Notes:

Pet Name:_____ Date of birth:_____

Breed:_____

Vaccine	Immunization Dates						Veterinarian
Ardenovirus-2							
Bordetella							
Coronavirus							
Distemper							
Heartworm							
Hepatitis							
Leptospirosis							
Lyme Disease							
Parainfluenza							
Parvovirus							
Rabies							

Notes:

Pet Name:_____ Date of birth:_____

Breed:_____

Vaccine	Immunization Dates						Veterinarian
Ardenovirus-2							
Bordetella							
Coronavirus							
Distemper							
Heartworm							
Hepatitis							
Leptospirosis							
Lyme Disease							
Parainfluenza							
Parvovirus							
Rabies							

Notes:

Pet Name:_____ Date of birth:_____

Breed:_____

Vaccine	Immunization Dates						Veterinarian
Ardenovirus-2							
Bordetella							
Coronavirus							
Distemper							
Heartworm							
Hepatitis							
Leptospirosis							
Lyme Disease							
Parainfluenza							
Parvovirus							
Rabies							

Notes:

Pet Name:_____ Date of birth:_____

Breed:_____

Vaccine	Immunization Dates						Veterinarian
Ardenovirus-2							
Bordetella							
Coronavirus							
Distemper							
Heartworm							
Hepatitis							
Leptospirosis							
Lyme Disease							
Parainfluenza							
Parvovirus							
Rabies							

Notes:

Pet Name:_____ Date of birth:_____

Breed:_____

Vaccine	Immunization Dates						Veterinarian
Ardenovirus-2							
Bordetella							
Coronavirus							
Distemper							
Heartworm							
Hepatitis							
Leptospirosis							
Lyme Disease							
Parainfluenza							
Parvovirus							
Rabies							

Notes:

Pet Name:_____ Date of birth:_____

Breed:_____

Vaccine	Immunization Dates						Veterinarian
Ardenovirus-2							
Bordetella							
Coronavirus							
Distemper							
Heartworm							
Hepatitis							
Leptospirosis							
Lyme Disease							
Parainfluenza							
Parvovirus							
Rabies							

Notes:

Pet Name:_____ Date of birth:_____

Breed:_____

Vaccine	Immunization Dates						Veterinarian
Ardenovirus-2							
Bordetella							
Coronavirus							
Distemper							
Heartworm							
Hepatitis							
Leptospirosis							
Lyme Disease							
Parainfluenza							
Parvovirus							
Rabies							

Notes:

Pet Name:_____ Date of birth:_____

Breed:_____

Vaccine	Immunization Dates						Veterinarian
Ardenovirus-2							
Bordetella							
Coronavirus							
Distemper							
Heartworm							
Hepatitis							
Leptospirosis							
Lyme Disease							
Parainfluenza							
Parvovirus							
Rabies							

Notes:

Pet Name:_____ Date of birth:_____

Breed:_____

Vaccine	Immunization Dates						Veterinarian
Ardenovirus-2							
Bordetella							
Coronavirus							
Distemper							
Heartworm							
Hepatitis							
Leptospirosis							
Lyme Disease							
Parainfluenza							
Parvovirus							
Rabies							

Notes:

Pet Name:_____ Date of birth:_____

Breed:_____

Vaccine	Immunization Dates					Veterinarian
Ardenovirus-2						
Bordetella						
Coronavirus						
Distemper						
Heartworm						
Hepatitis						
Leptospirosis						
Lyme Disease						
Parainfluenza						
Parvovirus						
Rabies						

Notes:

Pet Name:_____ Date of birth:_____

Breed:_____

Vaccine	Immunization Dates						Veterinarian
Ardenovirus-2							
Bordetella							
Coronavirus							
Distemper							
Heartworm							
Hepatitis							
Leptospirosis							
Lyme Disease							
Parainfluenza							
Parvovirus							
Rabies							

Notes:

Pet Name:_____ Date of birth:_____

Breed:_____

Vaccine	Immunization Dates						Veterinarian
Ardenovirus-2							
Bordetella							
Coronavirus							
Distemper							
Heartworm							
Hepatitis							
Leptospirosis							
Lyme Disease							
Parainfluenza							
Parvovirus							
Rabies							

Notes:

Pet Name:_____ Date of birth:_____

Breed:_____

Vaccine	Immunization Dates						Veterinarian
Ardenovirus-2							
Bordetella							
Coronavirus							
Distemper							
Heartworm							
Hepatitis							
Leptospirosis							
Lyme Disease							
Parainfluenza							
Parvovirus							
Rabies							

Notes:

Pet Name:_____ Date of birth:_____

Breed:_____

Vaccine	Immunization Dates						Veterinarian
Ardenovirus-2							
Bordetella							
Coronavirus							
Distemper							
Heartworm							
Hepatitis							
Leptospirosis							
Lyme Disease							
Parainfluenza							
Parvovirus							
Rabies							

Notes:

Pet Name:_____ Date of birth:_____

Breed:_____

Vaccine	Immunization Dates						Veterinarian
Ardenovirus-2							
Bordetella							
Coronavirus							
Distemper							
Heartworm							
Hepatitis							
Leptospirosis							
Lyme Disease							
Parainfluenza							
Parvovirus							
Rabies							

Notes:

Pet Name:_____ Date of birth:_____

Breed:_____

Vaccine	Immunization Dates						Veterinarian
Ardenovirus-2							
Bordetella							
Coronavirus							
Distemper							
Heartworm							
Hepatitis							
Leptospirosis							
Lyme Disease							
Parainfluenza							
Parvovirus							
Rabies							

Notes:

Pet Name:_____ Date of birth:_____

Breed:_____

Vaccine	Immunization Dates						Veterinarian
Ardenovirus-2							
Bordetella							
Coronavirus							
Distemper							
Heartworm							
Hepatitis							
Leptospirosis							
Lyme Disease							
Parainfluenza							
Parvovirus							
Rabies							

Notes:

Pet Name:_____ Date of birth:_____

Breed:_____

Vaccine	Immunization Dates						Veterinarian
Ardenovirus-2							
Bordetella							
Coronavirus							
Distemper							
Heartworm							
Hepatitis							
Leptospirosis							
Lyme Disease							
Parainfluenza							
Parvovirus							
Rabies							

Notes:

Pet Name:_____ Date of birth:_____

Breed:_____

Vaccine	Immunization Dates						Veterinarian
Ardenovirus-2							
Bordetella							
Coronavirus							
Distemper							
Heartworm							
Hepatitis							
Leptospirosis							
Lyme Disease							
Parainfluenza							
Parvovirus							
Rabies							

Notes:

Pet Name:_____ Date of birth:_____

Breed:_____

Vaccine	Immunization Dates						Veterinarian
Ardenovirus-2							
Bordetella							
Coronavirus							
Distemper							
Heartworm							
Hepatitis							
Leptospirosis							
Lyme Disease							
Parainfluenza							
Parvovirus							
Rabies							

Notes:

Pet Name:_____ Date of birth:_____

Breed:_____

Vaccine	Immunization Dates						Veterinarian
Ardenovirus-2							
Bordetella							
Coronavirus							
Distemper							
Heartworm							
Hepatitis							
Leptospirosis							
Lyme Disease							
Parainfluenza							
Parvovirus							
Rabies							

Notes:

Pet Name:_____ Date of birth:_____

Breed:_____

Vaccine	Immunization Dates						Veterinarian
Ardenovirus-2							
Bordetella							
Coronavirus							
Distemper							
Heartworm							
Hepatitis							
Leptospirosis							
Lyme Disease							
Parainfluenza							
Parvovirus							
Rabies							

Notes:

Pet Name:_____ Date of birth:_____

Breed:_____

Vaccine	Immunization Dates						Veterinarian
Ardenovirus-2							
Bordetella							
Coronavirus							
Distemper							
Heartworm							
Hepatitis							
Leptospirosis							
Lyme Disease							
Parainfluenza							
Parvovirus							
Rabies							

Notes:

Pet Name:_____ Date of birth:_____

Breed:_____

Vaccine	Immunization Dates						Veterinarian
Ardenovirus-2							
Bordetella							
Coronavirus							
Distemper							
Heartworm							
Hepatitis							
Leptospirosis							
Lyme Disease							
Parainfluenza							
Parvovirus							
Rabies							

Notes:

Pet Name:_____ Date of birth:_____

Breed:_____

Vaccine	Immunization Dates						Veterinarian
Ardenovirus-2							
Bordetella							
Coronavirus							
Distemper							
Heartworm							
Hepatitis							
Leptospirosis							
Lyme Disease							
Parainfluenza							
Parvovirus							
Rabies							

Notes:

Pet Name:_____ Date of birth:_____

Breed:_____

Vaccine	Immunization Dates						Veterinarian
Ardenovirus-2							
Bordetella							
Coronavirus							
Distemper							
Heartworm							
Hepatitis							
Leptospirosis							
Lyme Disease							
Parainfluenza							
Parvovirus							
Rabies							

Notes:

Pet Name:_____ Date of birth:_____

Breed:_____

Vaccine	Immunization Dates						Veterinarian
Ardenovirus-2							
Bordetella							
Coronavirus							
Distemper							
Heartworm							
Hepatitis							
Leptospirosis							
Lyme Disease							
Parainfluenza							
Parvovirus							
Rabies							

Notes:

Pet Name:_____ Date of birth:_____

Breed:_____

Vaccine	Immunization Dates						Veterinarian
Ardenovirus-2							
Bordetella							
Coronavirus							
Distemper							
Heartworm							
Hepatitis							
Leptospirosis							
Lyme Disease							
Parainfluenza							
Parvovirus							
Rabies							

Notes:

Pet Name:_____ Date of birth:_____

Breed:_____

Vaccine	Immunization Dates						Veterinarian
Ardenovirus-2							
Bordetella							
Coronavirus							
Distemper							
Heartworm							
Hepatitis							
Leptospirosis							
Lyme Disease							
Parainfluenza							
Parvovirus							
Rabies							

Notes:

Pet Name:_____ Date of birth:_____

Breed:_____

Vaccine	Immunization Dates						Veterinarian
Ardenovirus-2							
Bordetella							
Coronavirus							
Distemper							
Heartworm							
Hepatitis							
Leptospirosis							
Lyme Disease							
Parainfluenza							
Parvovirus							
Rabies							

Notes:

Pet Name:_____   Date of birth:_____

Breed:_____

Vaccine	Immunization Dates						Veterinarian
Ardenovirus-2							
Bordetella							
Coronavirus							
Distemper							
Heartworm							
Hepatitis							
Leptospirosis							
Lyme Disease							
Parainfluenza							
Parvovirus							
Rabies							

Notes:

Pet Name:_____ Date of birth:_____

Breed:_____

Vaccine	Immunization Dates						Veterinarian
Ardenovirus-2							
Bordetella							
Coronavirus							
Distemper							
Heartworm							
Hepatitis							
Leptospirosis							
Lyme Disease							
Parainfluenza							
Parvovirus							
Rabies							

Notes:

Pet Name:_____ Date of birth:_____

Breed:_____

Vaccine	Immunization Dates						Veterinarian
Ardenovirus-2							
Bordetella							
Coronavirus							
Distemper							
Heartworm							
Hepatitis							
Leptospirosis							
Lyme Disease							
Parainfluenza							
Parvovirus							
Rabies							

Notes:

Pet Name:_____ Date of birth:_____

Breed:_____

Vaccine	Immunization Dates						Veterinarian
Ardenovirus-2							
Bordetella							
Coronavirus							
Distemper							
Heartworm							
Hepatitis							
Leptospirosis							
Lyme Disease							
Parainfluenza							
Parvovirus							
Rabies							

Notes:

Pet Name:_____ Date of birth:_____

Breed:_____

Vaccine	Immunization Dates						Veterinarian
Ardenovirus-2							
Bordetella							
Coronavirus							
Distemper							
Heartworm							
Hepatitis							
Leptospirosis							
Lyme Disease							
Parainfluenza							
Parvovirus							
Rabies							

Notes:

Pet Name:_____ Date of birth:_____

Breed:_____

Vaccine	Immunization Dates						Veterinarian
Ardenovirus-2							
Bordetella							
Coronavirus							
Distemper							
Heartworm							
Hepatitis							
Leptospirosis							
Lyme Disease							
Parainfluenza							
Parvovirus							
Rabies							

Notes:

Pet Name:_____ Date of birth:_____

Breed:_____

Vaccine	Immunization Dates						Veterinarian
Ardenovirus-2							
Bordetella							
Coronavirus							
Distemper							
Heartworm							
Hepatitis							
Leptospirosis							
Lyme Disease							
Parainfluenza							
Parvovirus							
Rabies							

Notes:

Pet Name:_____ Date of birth:_____

Breed:_____

Vaccine	Immunization Dates						Veterinarian
Ardenovirus-2							
Bordetella							
Coronavirus							
Distemper							
Heartworm							
Hepatitis							
Leptospirosis							
Lyme Disease							
Parainfluenza							
Parvovirus							
Rabies							

Notes:

Pet Name:_____ Date of birth:_____

Breed:_____

Vaccine	Immunization Dates						Veterinarian
Ardenovirus-2							
Bordetella							
Coronavirus							
Distemper							
Heartworm							
Hepatitis							
Leptospirosis							
Lyme Disease							
Parainfluenza							
Parvovirus							
Rabies							

Notes:

Pet Name:_____ Date of birth:_____

Breed:_____

Vaccine	Immunization Dates						Veterinarian
Ardenovirus-2							
Bordetella							
Coronavirus							
Distemper							
Heartworm							
Hepatitis							
Leptospirosis							
Lyme Disease							
Parainfluenza							
Parvovirus							
Rabies							

Notes:

Pet Name:_____ Date of birth:_____

Breed:_____

Vaccine	Immunization Dates						Veterinarian
Ardenovirus-2							
Bordetella							
Coronavirus							
Distemper							
Heartworm							
Hepatitis							
Leptospirosis							
Lyme Disease							
Parainfluenza							
Parvovirus							
Rabies							

Notes:

Pet Name:_____ Date of birth:_____

Breed:_____

Vaccine	Immunization Dates						Veterinarian
Ardenovirus-2							
Bordetella							
Coronavirus							
Distemper							
Heartworm							
Hepatitis							
Leptospirosis							
Lyme Disease							
Parainfluenza							
Parvovirus							
Rabies							

Notes:

Pet Name:_____ Date of birth:_____

Breed:_____

Vaccine	Immunization Dates						Veterinarian
Ardenovirus-2							
Bordetella							
Coronavirus							
Distemper							
Heartworm							
Hepatitis							
Leptospirosis							
Lyme Disease							
Parainfluenza							
Parvovirus							
Rabies							

Notes:

Pet Name:_____ Date of birth:_____

Breed:_____

Vaccine	Immunization Dates						Veterinarian
Ardenovirus-2							
Bordetella							
Coronavirus							
Distemper							
Heartworm							
Hepatitis							
Leptospirosis							
Lyme Disease							
Parainfluenza							
Parvovirus							
Rabies							

Notes:

Pet Name:_____ Date of birth:_____

Breed:_____

Vaccine	Immunization Dates						Veterinarian
Ardenovirus-2							
Bordetella							
Coronavirus							
Distemper							
Heartworm							
Hepatitis							
Leptospirosis							
Lyme Disease							
Parainfluenza							
Parvovirus							
Rabies							

Notes:

Pet Name:_____ Date of birth:_____

Breed:_____

Vaccine	Immunization Dates						Veterinarian
Ardenovirus-2							
Bordetella							
Coronavirus							
Distemper							
Heartworm							
Hepatitis							
Leptospirosis							
Lyme Disease							
Parainfluenza							
Parvovirus							
Rabies							

Notes:

Pet Name:_____   Date of birth:_____

Breed:_____

Vaccine	Immunization Dates						Veterinarian
Ardenovirus-2							
Bordetella							
Coronavirus							
Distemper							
Heartworm							
Hepatitis							
Leptospirosis							
Lyme Disease							
Parainfluenza							
Parvovirus							
Rabies							

Notes:

Pet Name:_____ Date of birth:_____

Breed:_____

Vaccine	Immunization Dates						Veterinarian
Ardenovirus-2							
Bordetella							
Coronavirus							
Distemper							
Heartworm							
Hepatitis							
Leptospirosis							
Lyme Disease							
Parainfluenza							
Parvovirus							
Rabies							

Notes:

Pet Name:_____ Date of birth:_____

Breed:_____

Vaccine	Immunization Dates						Veterinarian
Ardenovirus-2							
Bordetella							
Coronavirus							
Distemper							
Heartworm							
Hepatitis							
Leptospirosis							
Lyme Disease							
Parainfluenza							
Parvovirus							
Rabies							

Notes:

Pet Name:_____ Date of birth:_____

Breed:_____

Vaccine	Immunization Dates						Veterinarian
Ardenovirus-2							
Bordetella							
Coronavirus							
Distemper							
Heartworm							
Hepatitis							
Leptospirosis							
Lyme Disease							
Parainfluenza							
Parvovirus							
Rabies							

Notes:

Pet Name:_____ Date of birth:_____

Breed:_____

Vaccine	Immunization Dates						Veterinarian
Ardenovirus-2							
Bordetella							
Coronavirus							
Distemper							
Heartworm							
Hepatitis							
Leptospirosis							
Lyme Disease							
Parainfluenza							
Parvovirus							
Rabies							

Notes:

Pet Name:_____ Date of birth:_____

Breed:_____

Vaccine	Immunization Dates						Veterinarian
Ardenovirus-2							
Bordetella							
Coronavirus							
Distemper							
Heartworm							
Hepatitis							
Leptospirosis							
Lyme Disease							
Parainfluenza							
Parvovirus							
Rabies							

Notes:

Pet Name:_____   Date of birth:_____

Breed:_____

Vaccine	Immunization Dates						Veterinarian
Ardenovirus-2							
Bordetella							
Coronavirus							
Distemper							
Heartworm							
Hepatitis							
Leptospirosis							
Lyme Disease							
Parainfluenza							
Parvovirus							
Rabies							

Notes:

Pet Name:_____   Date of birth:_____

Breed:_____

Vaccine	Immunization Dates						Veterinarian
Ardenovirus-2							
Bordetella							
Coronavirus							
Distemper							
Heartworm							
Hepatitis							
Leptospirosis							
Lyme Disease							
Parainfluenza							
Parvovirus							
Rabies							

Notes:

Pet Name:_____ Date of birth:_____

Breed:_____

Vaccine	Immunization Dates						Veterinarian
Ardenovirus-2							
Bordetella							
Coronavirus							
Distemper							
Heartworm							
Hepatitis							
Leptospirosis							
Lyme Disease							
Parainfluenza							
Parvovirus							
Rabies							

Notes:

Pet Name:_____ Date of birth:_____

Breed:_____

Vaccine	Immunization Dates						Veterinarian
Ardenovirus-2							
Bordetella							
Coronavirus							
Distemper							
Heartworm							
Hepatitis							
Leptospirosis							
Lyme Disease							
Parainfluenza							
Parvovirus							
Rabies							

Notes:

Pet Name:_____ Date of birth:_____

Breed:_____

Vaccine	Immunization Dates						Veterinarian
Ardenovirus-2							
Bordetella							
Coronavirus							
Distemper							
Heartworm							
Hepatitis							
Leptospirosis							
Lyme Disease							
Parainfluenza							
Parvovirus							
Rabies							

Notes:

Pet Name:_____ Date of birth:_____

Breed:_____

Vaccine	Immunization Dates						Veterinarian
Ardenovirus-2							
Bordetella							
Coronavirus							
Distemper							
Heartworm							
Hepatitis							
Leptospirosis							
Lyme Disease							
Parainfluenza							
Parvovirus							
Rabies							

Notes:

Pet Name:_____ Date of birth:_____

Breed:_____

Vaccine	Immunization Dates						Veterinarian
Ardenovirus-2							
Bordetella							
Coronavirus							
Distemper							
Heartworm							
Hepatitis							
Leptospirosis							
Lyme Disease							
Parainfluenza							
Parvovirus							
Rabies							

Notes:

Pet Name:_____ Date of birth:_____

Breed:_____

Vaccine	Immunization Dates						Veterinarian
Ardenovirus-2							
Bordetella							
Coronavirus							
Distemper							
Heartworm							
Hepatitis							
Leptospirosis							
Lyme Disease							
Parainfluenza							
Parvovirus							
Rabies							

Notes:

Pet Name:_____ Date of birth:_____

Breed:_____

Vaccine	Immunization Dates						Veterinarian
Ardenovirus-2							
Bordetella							
Coronavirus							
Distemper							
Heartworm							
Hepatitis							
Leptospirosis							
Lyme Disease							
Parainfluenza							
Parvovirus							
Rabies							

Notes:

Pet Name:_____ Date of birth:_____

Breed:_____

Vaccine	Immunization Dates						Veterinarian
Ardenovirus-2							
Bordetella							
Coronavirus							
Distemper							
Heartworm							
Hepatitis							
Leptospirosis							
Lyme Disease							
Parainfluenza							
Parvovirus							
Rabies							

Notes:

Pet Name:_____ Date of birth:_____

Breed:_____

Vaccine	Immunization Dates						Veterinarian
Ardenovirus-2							
Bordetella							
Coronavirus							
Distemper							
Heartworm							
Hepatitis							
Leptospirosis							
Lyme Disease							
Parainfluenza							
Parvovirus							
Rabies							

Notes:

Pet Name:_____ Date of birth:_____

Breed:_____

Vaccine	Immunization Dates						Veterinarian
Ardenovirus-2							
Bordetella							
Coronavirus							
Distemper							
Heartworm							
Hepatitis							
Leptospirosis							
Lyme Disease							
Parainfluenza							
Parvovirus							
Rabies							

Notes:

Pet Name:_____ Date of birth:_____

Breed:_____

Vaccine	Immunization Dates						Veterinarian
Ardenovirus-2							
Bordetella							
Coronavirus							
Distemper							
Heartworm							
Hepatitis							
Leptospirosis							
Lyme Disease							
Parainfluenza							
Parvovirus							
Rabies							

Notes:

Pet Name:_____ Date of birth:_____

Breed:_____

Vaccine	Immunization Dates						Veterinarian
Ardenovirus-2							
Bordetella							
Coronavirus							
Distemper							
Heartworm							
Hepatitis							
Leptospirosis							
Lyme Disease							
Parainfluenza							
Parvovirus							
Rabies							

Notes:

Pet Name:_____ Date of birth:_____

Breed:_____

Vaccine	Immunization Dates						Veterinarian
Ardenovirus-2							
Bordetella							
Coronavirus							
Distemper							
Heartworm							
Hepatitis							
Leptospirosis							
Lyme Disease							
Parainfluenza							
Parvovirus							
Rabies							

Notes:

Pet Name:_____ Date of birth:_____

Breed:_____

Vaccine	Immunization Dates						Veterinarian
Ardenovirus-2							
Bordetella							
Coronavirus							
Distemper							
Heartworm							
Hepatitis							
Leptospirosis							
Lyme Disease							
Parainfluenza							
Parvovirus							
Rabies							

Notes:

Pet Name:_____ Date of birth:_____

Breed:_____

Vaccine	Immunization Dates						Veterinarian
Ardenovirus-2							
Bordetella							
Coronavirus							
Distemper							
Heartworm							
Hepatitis							
Leptospirosis							
Lyme Disease							
Parainfluenza							
Parvovirus							
Rabies							

Notes:

Pet Name:_____ Date of birth:_____

Breed:_____

Vaccine	Immunization Dates						Veterinarian
Ardenovirus-2							
Bordetella							
Coronavirus							
Distemper							
Heartworm							
Hepatitis							
Leptospirosis							
Lyme Disease							
Parainfluenza							
Parvovirus							
Rabies							

Notes:

Pet Name:_____ Date of birth:_____

Breed:_____

Vaccine	Immunization Dates						Veterinarian
Ardenovirus-2							
Bordetella							
Coronavirus							
Distemper							
Heartworm							
Hepatitis							
Leptospirosis							
Lyme Disease							
Parainfluenza							
Parvovirus							
Rabies							

Notes:

Pet Name:_____ Date of birth:_____

Breed:_____

Vaccine	Immunization Dates						Veterinarian
Ardenovirus-2							
Bordetella							
Coronavirus							
Distemper							
Heartworm							
Hepatitis							
Leptospirosis							
Lyme Disease							
Parainfluenza							
Parvovirus							
Rabies							

Notes:

Pet Name:_____ Date of birth:_____

Breed:_____

Vaccine	Immunization Dates						Veterinarian
Ardenovirus-2							
Bordetella							
Coronavirus							
Distemper							
Heartworm							
Hepatitis							
Leptospirosis							
Lyme Disease							
Parainfluenza							
Parvovirus							
Rabies							

Notes:

Pet Name:_____ Date of birth:_____

Breed:_____

Vaccine	Immunization Dates						Veterinarian
Ardenovirus-2							
Bordetella							
Coronavirus							
Distemper							
Heartworm							
Hepatitis							
Leptospirosis							
Lyme Disease							
Parainfluenza							
Parvovirus							
Rabies							

Notes:

Pet Name:_____ Date of birth:_____

Breed:_____

Vaccine	Immunization Dates						Veterinarian
Ardenovirus-2							
Bordetella							
Coronavirus							
Distemper							
Heartworm							
Hepatitis							
Leptospirosis							
Lyme Disease							
Parainfluenza							
Parvovirus							
Rabies							

Notes:

Pet Name:_____ Date of birth:_____

Breed:_____

Vaccine	Immunization Dates						Veterinarian
Ardenovirus-2							
Bordetella							
Coronavirus							
Distemper							
Heartworm							
Hepatitis							
Leptospirosis							
Lyme Disease							
Parainfluenza							
Parvovirus							
Rabies							

Notes:

Pet Name:_____ Date of birth:_____

Breed:_____

Vaccine	Immunization Dates						Veterinarian
Ardenovirus-2							
Bordetella							
Coronavirus							
Distemper							
Heartworm							
Hepatitis							
Leptospirosis							
Lyme Disease							
Parainfluenza							
Parvovirus							
Rabies							

Notes:

Pet Name:_____ Date of birth:_____

Breed:_____

Vaccine	Immunization Dates						Veterinarian
Ardenovirus-2							
Bordetella							
Coronavirus							
Distemper							
Heartworm							
Hepatitis							
Leptospirosis							
Lyme Disease							
Parainfluenza							
Parvovirus							
Rabies							

Notes:

Pet Name:_____ Date of birth:_____

Breed:_____

Vaccine	Immunization Dates						Veterinarian
Ardenovirus-2							
Bordetella							
Coronavirus							
Distemper							
Heartworm							
Hepatitis							
Leptospirosis							
Lyme Disease							
Parainfluenza							
Parvovirus							
Rabies							

Notes:

Pet Name:_____ Date of birth:_____

Breed:_____

Vaccine	Immunization Dates						Veterinarian
Ardenovirus-2							
Bordetella							
Coronavirus							
Distemper							
Heartworm							
Hepatitis							
Leptospirosis							
Lyme Disease							
Parainfluenza							
Parvovirus							
Rabies							

Notes:

Pet Name:_____ Date of birth:_____

Breed:_____

Vaccine	Immunization Dates						Veterinarian
Ardenovirus-2							
Bordetella							
Coronavirus							
Distemper							
Heartworm							
Hepatitis							
Leptospirosis							
Lyme Disease							
Parainfluenza							
Parvovirus							
Rabies							

Notes:

Pet Name:_____ Date of birth:_____

Breed:_____

Vaccine	Immunization Dates						Veterinarian
Ardenovirus-2							
Bordetella							
Coronavirus							
Distemper							
Heartworm							
Hepatitis							
Leptospirosis							
Lyme Disease							
Parainfluenza							
Parvovirus							
Rabies							

Notes:

Pet Name:_____ Date of birth:_____

Breed:_____

Vaccine	Immunization Dates						Veterinarian
Ardenovirus-2							
Bordetella							
Coronavirus							
Distemper							
Heartworm							
Hepatitis							
Leptospirosis							
Lyme Disease							
Parainfluenza							
Parvovirus							
Rabies							

Notes:

Pet Name:_____ Date of birth:_____

Breed:_____

Vaccine	Immunization Dates						Veterinarian
Ardenovirus-2							
Bordetella							
Coronavirus							
Distemper							
Heartworm							
Hepatitis							
Leptospirosis							
Lyme Disease							
Parainfluenza							
Parvovirus							
Rabies							

Notes:

Pet Name:_____ Date of birth:_____

Breed:_____

Vaccine	Immunization Dates						Veterinarian
Ardenovirus-2							
Bordetella							
Coronavirus							
Distemper							
Heartworm							
Hepatitis							
Leptospirosis							
Lyme Disease							
Parainfluenza							
Parvovirus							
Rabies							

Notes:

Pet Name:_____ Date of birth:_____

Breed:_____

Vaccine	Immunization Dates						Veterinarian
Ardenovirus-2							
Bordetella							
Coronavirus							
Distemper							
Heartworm							
Hepatitis							
Leptospirosis							
Lyme Disease							
Parainfluenza							
Parvovirus							
Rabies							

Notes:

Pet Name:_____ Date of birth:_____

Breed:_____

Vaccine	Immunization Dates						Veterinarian
Ardenovirus-2							
Bordetella							
Coronavirus							
Distemper							
Heartworm							
Hepatitis							
Leptospirosis							
Lyme Disease							
Parainfluenza							
Parvovirus							
Rabies							

Notes:

Pet Name:_____ Date of birth:_____

Breed:_____

Vaccine	Immunization Dates						Veterinarian
Ardenovirus-2							
Bordetella							
Coronavirus							
Distemper							
Heartworm							
Hepatitis							
Leptospirosis							
Lyme Disease							
Parainfluenza							
Parvovirus							
Rabies							

Notes:

Pet Name:_____ Date of birth:_____

Breed:_____

Vaccine	Immunization Dates						Veterinarian
Ardenovirus-2							
Bordetella							
Coronavirus							
Distemper							
Heartworm							
Hepatitis							
Leptospirosis							
Lyme Disease							
Parainfluenza							
Parvovirus							
Rabies							

Notes:

Pet Name:_____ Date of birth:_____

Breed:_____

Vaccine	Immunization Dates						Veterinarian
Ardenovirus-2							
Bordetella							
Coronavirus							
Distemper							
Heartworm							
Hepatitis							
Leptospirosis							
Lyme Disease							
Parainfluenza							
Parvovirus							
Rabies							

Notes:

Pet Name:_____ Date of birth:_____

Breed:_____

Vaccine	Immunization Dates						Veterinarian
Ardenovirus-2							
Bordetella							
Coronavirus							
Distemper							
Heartworm							
Hepatitis							
Leptospirosis							
Lyme Disease							
Parainfluenza							
Parvovirus							
Rabies							

Notes:

Pet Name:_____ Date of birth:_____

Breed:_____

Vaccine	Immunization Dates						Veterinarian
Ardenovirus-2							
Bordetella							
Coronavirus							
Distemper							
Heartworm							
Hepatitis							
Leptospirosis							
Lyme Disease							
Parainfluenza							
Parvovirus							
Rabies							

Notes:

Pet Name:_____ Date of birth:_____

Breed:_____

Vaccine	Immunization Dates						Veterinarian
Ardenovirus-2							
Bordetella							
Coronavirus							
Distemper							
Heartworm							
Hepatitis							
Leptospirosis							
Lyme Disease							
Parainfluenza							
Parvovirus							
Rabies							

Notes:

Pet Name:_____ Date of birth:_____

Breed:_____

Vaccine	Immunization Dates						Veterinarian
Ardenovirus-2							
Bordetella							
Coronavirus							
Distemper							
Heartworm							
Hepatitis							
Leptospirosis							
Lyme Disease							
Parainfluenza							
Parvovirus							
Rabies							

Notes:

Pet Name:_____ Date of birth:_____

Breed:_____

Vaccine	Immunization Dates						Veterinarian
Ardenovirus-2							
Bordetella							
Coronavirus							
Distemper							
Heartworm							
Hepatitis							
Leptospirosis							
Lyme Disease							
Parainfluenza							
Parvovirus							
Rabies							

Notes:

Pet Name:_____ Date of birth:_____

Breed:_____

Vaccine	Immunization Dates						Veterinarian
Ardenovirus-2							
Bordetella							
Coronavirus							
Distemper							
Heartworm							
Hepatitis							
Leptospirosis							
Lyme Disease							
Parainfluenza							
Parvovirus							
Rabies							

Notes:

Pet Name:_____ Date of birth:_____

Breed:_____

Vaccine	Immunization Dates						Veterinarian
Ardenovirus-2							
Bordetella							
Coronavirus							
Distemper							
Heartworm							
Hepatitis							
Leptospirosis							
Lyme Disease							
Parainfluenza							
Parvovirus							
Rabies							

Notes:

Pet Name:_____ Date of birth:_____

Breed:_____

Vaccine	Immunization Dates						Veterinarian
Ardenovirus-2							
Bordetella							
Coronavirus							
Distemper							
Heartworm							
Hepatitis							
Leptospirosis							
Lyme Disease							
Parainfluenza							
Parvovirus							
Rabies							

Notes:

Pet Name:_____ Date of birth:_____

Breed:_____

Vaccine	Immunization Dates						Veterinarian
Ardenovirus-2							
Bordetella							
Coronavirus							
Distemper							
Heartworm							
Hepatitis							
Leptospirosis							
Lyme Disease							
Parainfluenza							
Parvovirus							
Rabies							

Notes:

Pet Name:_____ Date of birth:_____

Breed:_____

Vaccine	Immunization Dates						Veterinarian
Ardenovirus-2							
Bordetella							
Coronavirus							
Distemper							
Heartworm							
Hepatitis							
Leptospirosis							
Lyme Disease							
Parainfluenza							
Parvovirus							
Rabies							

Notes:

Pet Name:_____ Date of birth:_____

Breed:_____

Vaccine	Immunization Dates						Veterinarian
Ardenovirus-2							
Bordetella							
Coronavirus							
Distemper							
Heartworm							
Hepatitis							
Leptospirosis							
Lyme Disease							
Parainfluenza							
Parvovirus							
Rabies							

Notes:

Pet Name:_____ Date of birth:_____

Breed:_____

Vaccine	Immunization Dates						Veterinarian
Ardenovirus-2							
Bordetella							
Coronavirus							
Distemper							
Heartworm							
Hepatitis							
Leptospirosis							
Lyme Disease							
Parainfluenza							
Parvovirus							
Rabies							

Notes:

Pet Name:_____ Date of birth:_____

Breed:_____

Vaccine	Immunization Dates						Veterinarian
Ardenovirus-2							
Bordetella							
Coronavirus							
Distemper							
Heartworm							
Hepatitis							
Leptospirosis							
Lyme Disease							
Parainfluenza							
Parvovirus							
Rabies							

Notes:

Pet Name:_____ Date of birth:_____

Breed:_____

Vaccine	Immunization Dates						Veterinarian
Ardenovirus-2							
Bordetella							
Coronavirus							
Distemper							
Heartworm							
Hepatitis							
Leptospirosis							
Lyme Disease							
Parainfluenza							
Parvovirus							
Rabies							

Notes:

Pet Name:_____ Date of birth:_____

Breed:_____

Vaccine	Immunization Dates						Veterinarian
Ardenovirus-2							
Bordetella							
Coronavirus							
Distemper							
Heartworm							
Hepatitis							
Leptospirosis							
Lyme Disease							
Parainfluenza							
Parvovirus							
Rabies							

Notes:

Pet Name:_____ Date of birth:_____

Breed:_____

Vaccine	Immunization Dates						Veterinarian
Ardenovirus-2							
Bordetella							
Coronavirus							
Distemper							
Heartworm							
Hepatitis							
Leptospirosis							
Lyme Disease							
Parainfluenza							
Parvovirus							
Rabies							

Notes: